D1612633

TOUCH WOOD

Other books by Isha Mellor

MY MOTHER SAID
MOTHER ALSO SAID

TOUCH WOOD

SUPERSTITIONS BY
ISHA MELLOR

ILLUSTRATED BY
RODNEY SHACKELL

W. H. ALLEN · LONDON
A Howard & Wyndham Company
1980

Printed and bound in Great Britain by
W & J Mackay Ltd, Chatham, Kent
for the Publishers, W. H. Allen & Co. Ltd,
44 Hill Street, London W1X 8LB

ISBN 0 491 02890 3

'There is a superstition in avoiding superstition.'
Francis Bacon

All my life I have wanted to find a four-leaved clover, but without success – until the day I completed the writing of this book.

Isha Mellor

CONTENTS

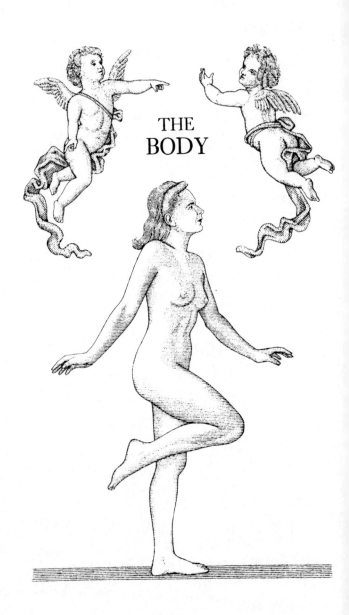

THE
BODY

THE BODY

I sometimes indulge in a fantasy that I find myself newly-born but fully-grown on a desert island. I imagine the slow realisation that I am a series of working parts, but wonder how long it will be before I open my eyes, move an arm, make a sound. How long will it be before I stand up, then walk? Shall I want to do so? There is no end to the questions, and the exercise has proved to be quite a good cure for insomnia.

Such a picture makes one understand how man may first have regarded his body. It felt well or ill, it moved in useful ways, the eyes and ears gave early warnings, very nasty accidents could happen to it at any moment, and there was the helplessness of infants and the aged. Anyone with a dangerous way of life is particularly aware of his body, and early life was always dangerous. The body's strength needed protection. With rather limited means of protection available, early man had to look elsewhere for assistance, to the spirits in the world 'up there'.

The science of medicine may simply have sprung from the realisation that cold spring water eased the pain of a sprained club-wielding wrist, or that the application of certain leaves grasped at random to mop up a wound made it heal more quickly.

The superstitions concerning fingers are very interesting, and it is easy to understand why, for we spend a lot of time using our hands and also simply looking at them as they lie idle. We note the differences in the length of fingers, in the right from the left, the shapes of the nails and the white spots that mysteriously appear on them and gradually work their way to the top. Man's passion for classification will have created the various qualities attributed to different fingers. We cross our fingers to cancel out effects of lies and dangers, seeking the good influence of the Cross. One has only to watch a Latin boarding a plane or going in for a swim to note the hasty little sign made over the breast. The lines on palms have given us an entire industry concerned with fortune-telling, and it is a fact that they do change in appearance during life.

The body does all kinds of funny things, like sneezing, hiccoughing, yawning, itching, losing teeth, and producing new moles. Why do these things happen? Can we control them? Are they warnings? Such questions conjure up strange reasons and precautions. Seldom can one sneeze without someone in earshot calling out 'Bless you'. Is it mere hygiene that makes us cover our mouths as we yawn? Does a sudden ringing in the ears or an itching palm signify something? We like to lean upon reasons, to memorise the little rhymes that list them. By the time we have remembered the part that applies to our particular affliction of the moment, the discomfort has usually vanished. Was it the power of the words? Or was it merely the fact that we were for a few moments distracted from scratching or rubbing? *Something* worked.

Fingers

Crossed fingers will cancel out the effects of a lie and will provide safety in dangerous situations. This is the basic holy sign, and is useful in its unobtrusiveness.

The index finger is poisonous and should never be used for rubbing in ointments. It used to be called the shooting finger, so it was not pleasant to have it pointed at one. Australian aborigines employ a menacing gesture called 'pointing the bone', and we now say it is rude to point.

The third finger has a nerve that runs through it right up to the heart. Wedding rings are worn on this finger because of this direct line to the seat of love and faithfulness. The Greeks and Romans referred to it as the medical finger, and used it for applying salves.

Fingernails

Cut your nails on a Sunday and you'll have the Devil with you all week. Cutting nails at sea brings up a storm. A woman who cuts her nails on the right hand with her left will be boss over her husband. Baby nails must not be cut during the first year but trimmed with mother's teeth; not to observe this will cause the child to grow into a thief. Nail parings must be carefully buried so they may not be used in spell recipes. All these ideas are based on the most common laws of superstition.

Tongue

A spot on the tongue indicates the recent telling of a lie. Biting it while eating is another sign of lying. It is impossible to ignore the pain caused, and because the tongue's big function is to speak, it is reasonable to suppose that the pain is a punishment for the lie.

Birthmarks

A child will be born with the mark on its face of the object or creature that frightened its mother during her pregnancy if she touches her face in an instinctive gesture of fear. A pregnant woman is therefore

schooled to clap her hands to her hips when suddenly
frightened, since a birthmark on the bottom is not
often likely to offend the eye. If the worst happens, the
baby's mark may be made to disappear if it is licked
by the mother each morning before she eats anything.

Milk teeth

When these fall out they should be placed under the
child's pillow for the angels. The substitution of
coins by loving parents is a sign that the angels have
taken the teeth into safe keeping. This is a custom
that comes from the universal precaution not to leave
any parings and suchlike from one's body lying
around to be used as material in witchcraft.

Caul

A sailor who carries a caul will never drown. Sailors,
who often cannot swim, are always on the lookout for
talismans, and what better than this curious membrane
from a newborn baby that as a foetus spent its life in
water?

Moles

A mole on the right side is a lucky mark, and particularly on the chin. One on the lip denotes fluency, and on the back of the neck an end on the gallows. The 18th century fashion of wearing black patches would have been a means of combining charm with charm.

Sneezing

A new baby remains under the influence of elves until it sneezes. No idiot can sneeze. It is lucky to sneeze to the right. Life has always been considered to be held in the breath, so an explosive sneeze might blow it right out. Hence the traditional 'Bless you'.

Itching

Right ear, your mother is thinking of you

Left ear, your lover

Right eye, pleasant surprise

Left eye, a disappointment

Right palm, money coming

Left palm, pay it out

Nose, you'll be kissed or shake hands with a fool

A sudden itching claims immediate attention. What does it signify? This rhyme sets it all out for us. It does seem hard that a lover is given the unpopular left side. He just isn't able to take precedence over formidable Mum!

Yawn

Cover your mouth when yawning or your soul may leave through your mouth or the Devil slip in while it remains wide open. There is only one yawn in the world and it goes round from person to person. Yawns are certainly catching (even as you read these words you will feel one coming on) and this is a neat explanation of the phenomenon.

The royal touch

The royal touch was given to cure scrofula. This was a French custom brought to this country by Edward the Confessor. Charles II touched nearly 100,000 sufferers but William III called it a silly superstition. It was last practised by Queen Anne on a most unlikely subject, Dr Johnson, without success.

Kissing

Kiss it better. This practice comes from the custom of sucking out poison from wounds. We have now progressed to giving the kiss of life, and this was most likely to have been the treatment that Sleeping Beauty received.

Hag stones

Crawling through a hag stone will cure lumbago. A small one hung round the neck will ward off witches or from the bedpost, nightmares and cramp. A hag stone is one with a natural hole right through it – an object of curiosity and magic. Crawling through will put one through contortions much like treatment given by osteopaths when they treat our aching backs.

Elbow

Your sex will change if you kiss your elbow. You will be quite safe in trying out this one. It is impossible.

Eyebrows

When eyebrows meet above the bridge of the nose their owner will never lack for money. Such eyebrows are also a sign of bad temper, and lifelong bachelorhood. The expression of determination they bestow has given rise to these beliefs.

Vitality

Indians are fearful of walking under telegraph wires or electric cables. They believe that their own vitality will be drawn out through their heads. If there is no way out of the situation, they wrap a cloth round their heads.

Chicken

A pregnant woman must never truss a fowl. To do so will cause her baby to be born with the cord wound round its neck.

CLOTHES

CLOTHES

As clothes evolved from the purely functional wrap of animal skins and became decorative, they assumed personal significance. Kings and priests wore robes embroidered with symbols to remind everyone who they were and what their functions were. Headdresses and crowns denoted rank and even in the commercial world practical headgear proclaimed one's trade. Not so very long ago carpenters wore square hats made out of newspaper to keep sawdust out of the hair, as we can see from Tenniel's drawing of the famous carpenter second only in fame to the young apprentice in Nazareth.

Gloves were employed as royal symbols and often sent with messengers as a kind of stand-in for the king who stayed safely at home. It was forbidden for anyone to appear before a king if wearing gloves, or to shake hands with them on. This was because they used to be quite loose fitting and therefore able to conceal a small dagger. A medieval knight would strike another with a glove as a challenge to fight, or simply throw it at his feet. If it was picked up the fight was on, and once arranged, each participant would send a glove as a pledge that he would attend to fight. This is why today we say it is bad luck to pick up a glove we have dropped, and further observe the rule not to thank the one who steps in to do this for us. We are still knights at heart, even if not spoiling for a fight.

It was the impressive ornamentation of clothes that made it a matter of note when a garment was accidentally put on inside out. It had to be worn for the rest of the day like that if the happy augury was not to be cancelled out. As a child I believed this implicitly and I was also told by a nurse that Friday was a very lucky day for this to happen. Whenever I put on that hated Liberty bodice (a misnomer if ever there was one) inside out, nothing would make me change it. All those buttons had to be done up from the inside, however late I was for school.

The clothes of those who have died are not readily accepted by the living. This is likely to be due to a fear of infection, and we are grateful to the various charities that will collect them for their good causes. Further back it was believed that a person's clothes could be used for the casting of spells, so they were not given away to strangers, however poor they might be.

The fashion trade has flourished on our instinct that what we wear presents to the world a view of what we are. Dressmakers and owners of dress shops are particularly superstitious, especially where bridal wear is concerned. One has to be careful with hats, shoes, petticoats, and hems, also about the wearing of green, and precious stones. It is considered safest only to wear one's actual birthstone, and lists of these are often included in the information pages of diaries, so there is no reason to plead ignorance if an opal does seem to have brought bad luck.

Dressing

Garments accidentally put on inside out must be kept that way, especially on a Friday, as it is a very lucky omen.

Clothes of the dead wear out quickly when given away. They mourn for their departed owner. We are sensitive about accepting such clothes, but tact forbids us to refuse and we tend to neglect them.

Mending clothes while someone is wearing them is unlucky because shrouds are the only things meant to be sewn on the body. To mend light materials with dark thread is also bad, but it is difficult to imagine why a superstition had to be thought up to prevent such a sluttish habit.

Buttons

Do not rootle in the button box for a replacement, but empty it all out. Failure to do this will mean that the freshly sewn on button will very quickly fall off.

Wearing green

It is unlucky to wear green. This is the colour of the 'little people'. To wear it is an invitation to elves and the like to add some mischief to the occasion. Actors are careful not to wear this colour unless the script calls for it.

Gloves

When you drop a glove, never pick it up yourself. When someone else does this for you, do not thank them. These rules hark back to medieval times when gloves were used in challenges to fight. One would hardly pick up one's own challenge.

Shoes

Tie an old shoe to the honeymoon car for luck. Anglo-Saxon daddy always gave one of the bride's shoes to the groom who then hit her on the head with it as a sign that authority over her had passed from father to husband. The poor girl never stood a chance !

Shoes must never be put on a table. This foretells a quarrel or death by hanging. The latter refers to the phrase 'to die in one's shoes', a term for hanging. The place for shoes is on the ground, if only for reasons of hygiene.

Shoes discarded at night with soles uppermost or in a T-form will keep away cramp and nightmares. To leave a pair crossed is not a good thing.

Sailor's collar

It is lucky to touch a sailor's collar, but it should be done without his noticing. Sailors are much bound up with superstitious thought, so we like to come under their influence. The secret touch is advisable if one considers the volatile nature of men who have spent so many days cooped up in ships. The habit is more prevalent in inland towns where a sailor is not such a common sight.

Hem

If the hem of a girl's dress is accidentally turned up it is a sign that her lover is thinking of her. She should kiss the hem and make a wish before turning it down.

23

Dress shops

Never roll up a tape measure in a dress shop. It looks as if one has given up hope of any more business that day. A rolled tape is no good to anyone. Never spin a coat hanger on its hook or allow empty hangers to rattle against each other on a rail. It is bad business to draw attention to low stocks.

A saleswoman not attracting much trade can have her luck changed by pinning onto herself two pins taken from a more successful colleague. We often state that 'for two pins' we will take certain action.

Owners of small dress shops will start the day by sweeping out into the street any pins left lying on the floor. The connection of pins with witchcraft will explain these actions.

Dressmakers

Sew a hair into the hem of a wedding dress for luck, or let a drop of blood fall onto an inner seam. Dressmakers, so often at the centre of the brouhaha of wedding preparations, use this physical method of attaching themselves to the traditional good fortune that attends a happy bride.

The bride must never try on the completed dress in advance of the wedding day. To this end a small section of the hem is left unsewn by the dressmaker

until the last moment. The bride must not be allowed
to tempt fate by presuming too much.

Bridal wear

Something old, something new
Something borrowed, something blue
And a lucky sixpence in her shoe.

The old and the new items will connect good influences
of the past with the present. Blue is the colour of
constancy and of the Virgin Mary. If the borrowed
item has belonged to a happily married women this
will carry good vibrations with it. The sixpence will
guarantee enough money through life.

The bride should not look at herself in a mirror in
her full array until the last possible moment before
leaving for the ceremony. Leaving off something like a
glove will suffice. This refers to the idea of the
reflected soul and is a precaution against the evil ones
being tempted to interfere. The veil is another
protection that is supposed to hide the bride. One way
of confusing the bad spirits is to pair off the Best Man
and the Chief Bridesmaid in the procession from the
church.

Laundry

Wash on Friday, wash in need
Wash on Saturday, a slut indeed.

These are the last lines of a verse mentioning every day of the week. The advice is a warning that it is best to do the family wash early in the week, with time for clothes to dry and air properly before being worn clean on Sunday.

Linen

A coffin (rectangular arrangement of creases) in a folded sheet means the occupant of the bed will soon die. In a tablecloth it means the death of someone who will sit at the table it covers. This is a simple pictorial warning not often to be found in our drip-dry sheets and table-mats.

Shrouds

Shrouds should only be made of linen. This is because Egyptians considered cloth woven from animal hair to be less pure than cloth made of plant fibres. Only the best was good enough for their dead, and one wonders what they would have thought of our man-made fibres.

Umbrella

Never open an umbrella inside the house, and if it is dropped let it be picked up by someone else. In the East, sunshades were used to cover royal heads only, and it was considered an insult to the Sun God to raise one in the shadow of trees (indoors). To drop a sunshade would have been an even greater insult, and a scapegoat would have had to be found.

All superstitions concerning sunshades have been transferred to umbrellas. These were not actually used in England until the 17th century, and then only by women. Jonas Hanway was much ridiculed when he became the first man to use one in the streets of London in 1778.

Purse

A purse given as a gift should contain a coin to make sure that it will never become empty.

Bird droppings

Good fortune will follow if a bird dropping falls on the shoulder. This idea has come about in a strange manner from the custom of always wearing new clothes at Easter; and that custom came from the

27

strewing of Lenten ashes that messed up any clothes worn at that time. Anyone not wearing new clothes on Easter Day would incur the disapproval of birds, who would drop their mark of displeasure on them. This happening now means quite the opposite.

Earrings

Pierced ears give good eyesight. When did you ever see a sailor with spectacles? His line of vision being bounded only by the far horizon keeps his eyes strong. The fact that he often wore gold earrings in pierced ears was a practical insurance policy: the gold could be used to pay for a decent burial on most foreign shores. The two factors – good sight plus pierced ears – have become linked.

Opals and pearls

Opals are unlucky and pearls mean tears. However, if these are your particular birthstones – October for opals and June for pearls – you are safeguarded, and in fact bestowed with happy influences. Most other birthstones may be worn with safety by anyone not born under the appropriate sign, but the October and June people seem to want to keep their good fortune to themselves.

Shoelace

When a shoelace comes undone of its own accord it shows that your lover is thinking about you.

Doorknob

Never hang a garment on a doorknob. It used, in some parts of the country, to be customary to hang a piece of clothing on the knob of the outer door to signify a death within. Naturally, it would be tempting fate to do so when no death had occurred.

Necklace

Witches hate the holy colour of blue, so it is a wise precaution to wear a necklace of blue beads.

Fringes

Bad spirits will become entangled in any fringes that are sewn on clothes, and so will be prevented from getting at the wearer.

ANIMALS

ANIMALS

Man's early neighbours, animals, were sources of food, clothing, locomotion, and protection. Birds, with their mystic ability to fly, were felt to be gods or messengers of gods. Fish provided nourishment, but to go after them men had to face the dangers of the sea. All hunters needed protection, apart from their weapons, and such protection took the form of rituals and observation of omens.

Magpies used to be tamed and kept in cages by entrances to farmyards because of their loud chattering at the approach of strangers. In this way they became associated with possible danger, with death. It is said that they refused to go into complete mourning at the time of the Crucifixion, and this is the reason for their white feathered streaks. We like birds to keep in their place, in the skies, and if they happen to come indoors it is not a good sign.

Animals behave in certain ways when changes in the weather are imminent. Shepherds who live so close to their woolly charges have noted and spoken about their behaviour, so we believe what we hear about red sky at night and red sky at morn.

Black does not have happy associations, so it is odd

31

that we feel pleased when a black cat crosses our path, and reasonable that in America, Belgium, and Spain a white cat is the lucky sign. Cats are happy to live close to humans and this has given rise to the belief that witches are able to enter into their bodies when they feel like it. The eccentric hare is also said to be used in this way.

Terrifying animals like sharks can start off legends. There is a Melanesian island where the inhabitants say that a person who escapes from the jaws of a shark will be infected with its horrible characteristics. These lie dormant until he happens to enter the sea, when he will turn murderously on anyone at hand. So firm is this belief that such a person has been known to flee to another island in order to escape the stigma and suspicion with which he is regarded.

Other creatures that live close to man, like horses, spiders, bees, and robins, carry their legends. It would be a bad thing if all spiders were killed on sight, so it is as well that we have rhymes to remind us of the time of day when they should be spared. Bees become strongly attached to their owners and like to be kept informed of all that happens in the family, particularly deaths. One may quite likely come across a hive with a piece of black cloth tied to it so that the inhabitants may join in the mourning. The robin perched on the handle of a gardener's spade is protected by the charming stories about the way it got its red breast.

He tried to draw a thorn out of the Crown of Thorns and the holy blood stained his front feathers. Also, in a charitable effort to relieve sufferers in Hell, he went to take them some water and got scorched for his trouble.

There is a nice story about the occasion when the Devil asked St Dunstan to shoe his single hoof. The Saint recognised the customer, tied him fast to the wall, and carried out his job as painfully as he could, making the Devil roar for mercy. He was released on condition that he promised never to enter a place where a horseshoe was displayed. This is why we see them above doors; and a further reason is the fact that they used to be made of iron, another talisman against evil.

Horse

Tangles in horses' manes are known as hag knots because witches can use them as stirrups when they take one of their free night rides. So those young girls who spend their time in stables lovingly grooming their charges are unknowingly beating the witches at their game!

Horseshoe

A horseshoe nailed to a house door will keep witches away. The ends of the shoe should point upwards so the lucky power can't run out.

Donkey

Riding on a donkey will cure many ills including whooping-cough and measles. This must be a popular remedy with children, particularly as it works better when the rider sits facing the tail. The donkey has a dark cross-shaped mark on its back, which will no doubt have credited it with healing powers. It is said that no one ever sees a dead donkey, but that such an exception brings outstanding good fortune.

Cat

A black cat crossing your path of its own accord is a very good sign in Britain. Sailors, while in favour of having a cat on board, will not pronounce the name at sea. If a cat passes a paw over its ear three times, rain will soon come. And there is a custom in which an illness can be got rid of by throwing water, in which the patient has been washed, over a cat and driving the unfortunate animal out of the house.

The independent nature of cats accentuates the beliefs about them, together with the fact that witches can assume their shapes. We remember also that the Egyptians had a cat-faced god and never allowed cats to be killed.

Hare

Bad luck will come if a hare crosses your path. Its flesh imparts melancholy when eaten. The child of a pregnant woman who sees a hare will be born with a hare lip. A hare's foot carried in the pocket was Samuel Pepys' certain cure for colic.

In pre-Christian times the hare was a sacred beast bound up with fertility and the return of Spring, and its flesh was not eaten by ordinary people. The Anglo-Saxon Spring Goddess was called Eastre, and from this we tell our children about the Easter Hare who lays the bright coloured eggs.

Sheep

When sheep lie down in a field it is a sign of good weather, and bad weather if they baa for no apparent reason. When I observe sheep they generally appear to be doing both these things, but I am quite prepared to accept any weather forecast a shepherd may make. To meet a flock of sheep on a road is fortunate – a tale surely meant to instil patience. A knucklebone from a sheep will keep rheumatism away if carried in the pocket. The compulsion to play with it provides a therapeutic exercise for keeping finger joints supple.

Magpies

One sorrow, two mirth
Three a wedding, four a birth
Five Heaven, six Hell
Seven the De'il's ain sell.

When meeting one magpie bow to it or spit or cross fingers. If a single one croaks persistently near the house it is an omen of death within.

Peacocks

The cry of a peacock is a sign of approaching rain, and the beautiful tail feathers will bring bad luck if brought into the house for decoration, because the 'eyes' are a reminder of the Evil Eye.

Cuckoo

Turn the money in your pocket when hearing the first cuckoo and you'll not want for it through the year. In Germany there is a cure for lumbago that entails rolling on the grass when the first cuckoo is heard, which must be good exercise for the back muscles. Employers wanting their servants up early in the morning will have supported the claim that bad luck follows if the strange call is heard while one is still in bed.

Robin

Misfortune will chase anyone who harms a robin or its nest. The bird's fearlessness close to humans, plus its unusual colouring, is likely to be the reason for legends attached to it, legends that make us love this friendly bird. 'A robin redbreast in a cage puts all Heaven in a rage.'

Fish

Eating fish will improve the brain. Scientists believed this to be true when they discovered that fish contained phosphorous which is also present in the brain. A fish should be eaten from the head to the tail as this gives power over the fish that remain in the sea, inducing them to swim towards the shore.

Fishermen sometimes throw one of their men into the water when the fish are not biting, believing that when he is dragged out again fish will follow him. They also consider it unwise to count the fish as they are caught because no more will come, and often the first fish out of the net is thrown back to go to his fellows and lure them to the boat.

Shark

A shark following a boat means that a death on board may be expected. They have an acute sense of smell for blood, and a wounded person in a boat can quite well attract the beast. In any event, the mere sight of it – the triangular fin, the backward pointing rows of teeth – will make most imaginations race in the direction of a terrible death.

Snail

Find one at dawn on May Day, put it on the hearth that still has log ash on it, and the trail left by the snail may be in the form of a letter signifying the initial of a future lover. If not, no lover for the rest of the year.

Bees

It is essential to tell the bees in the hive of every important event in the family. In the case of death, the eldest son should strike the hive three times with an iron key and make the announcement. Then black crêpe must be tied to the hive. When bees swarm after a beekeeper's death and are easily taken, it is a sign that they will accept their new master, but if they settle on dead wood he will not live long.

Bee stings are said to avert rheumatism, and even to cure it. It is a fact that beekeepers often remain free from this affliction throughout their lives.

Spiders

Araignée du matin, chagrin
Araignée du tantot, cadeau
Araignée du soir, espoir.

A nice summing up in French of what to expect from the appearance of a spider: in the morning – sorrow, at noon – a gift, in the evening – hope.

Most stories about spiders tell of friendly assistance to humans, from Robert the Bruce to the Holy Family on their flight into Egypt. Joseph hid them in a cave and a spider wove a web across the entrance so that pursuing soldiers seeing the unbroken web concluded that no one had entered.

FOOD

FOOD

Our appetites make us think constantly about food. Because a proper diet brings good rewards, and preparation takes so much time, it is worth taking it seriously. Scientists and the rudely termed 'food cranks' help to spread knowledge, but many people rely on superstitions to remind them of what should or should not be eaten, or how it should be treated. Much of this lore remains with us in the form of etiquette: the way we stir our tea, pass the salt, or throw away bread. Waste is considered very much to be a matter for guilt, so people with gardens and compost heaps enjoy having a good reason to collect kitchen waste.

One of the most famous mealtime superstitions relates to sitting thirteen to a table, because there was this number at the Last Supper. It is easy to pour scorn on the tale that death will soon come to one of the thirteen, but I was once present at a birthday party where eleven sat down to celebrate. Someone had the bright idea of inviting a lonely next door neighbour. She was pleased to accept but had a visitor staying with her. Naturally they were both told to come over. Two weeks later the neighbour's friend committed suicide. We look at such an event with hindsight and state that the suicide was contemplated before the invitation, that it had nothing to do with the number thirteen. Maybe not, but one cannot help wondering.

Bread is spoken of as the staff of life, and is closely related to Holy Communion. Pagans held it to be sacred because it belonged to the Corn Goddess who had to be worshipped and appeased if man was to survive. Eggs are an emblem of resurrection and the continuation of life, and for this reason have numerous superstitions surrounding them. Wedding cake represents fertility and good fortune, and is therefore made of the best and richest ingredients. It is offered to everyone so that the happy auras of bridal couples may shine on all the guests too.

When kings and high officials went in fear of poisoning, they employed tasters to take the first bite of each dish. I wonder if they were highly paid for this dangerous job, but imagine that the chance to sample *haute cuisine* every day was worth the risk anyway, particularly if one had some knowledge of antidotes.

Bread

It is wicked to burn bread. Roman Catholic children are told that it will make the Virgin Mary weep, and generally it is felt that it will cause hunger in later years. Only one person should put bread into the oven, neither should any other bread be cut while new bread is baking. A loaf should not be cut at both ends, nor be touched when another person is cutting it. To take the last slice from a dish is unlucky unless it is offered. In this case it foretells a handsome husband or ten thousand pounds a year.

These are but a few of the superstitions concerning bread, and they relate to the importance of its function in sustaining life, and also to its part in the sacrament of Holy Communion in which the priest is the only one to touch it during the transubstantiation.

Wedding cake

The first slice of a wedding cake should be cut by the bride or she will remain childless. If the groom's hand is placed on top of hers as she cuts, he will be the boss. Wedding guests are always ready to warn her about this danger. Everyone present must eat some of the cake. To refuse brings ill luck both to the newlyweds and the refuser. If girls put a piece of the cake under their pillows for three nights running they can expect to dream of future husbands. As if they're not always doing this!

Eggs

Smash your breakfast eggshell so no witch can use it as a boat. An egg laid on Good Friday will stay fresh for a year. Eggshells should never be burned on a farm or the hen that laid them will produce no more. Sailors say it is unlucky to buy eggs on board. These are all ideas that have come from the fact that an egg is the representation of life continuation.

Tea

If two women pour from the same teapot the second will have a baby within the year. Never stir a cup of tea with a knife or trouble will be stirred up. A stick of tea floating in a cup tells of a stranger's visit.

Gooseberry

Stewed gooseberries eaten on Whit Sunday will stop any tendency to make a fool of oneself during the year. From this custom we may have invented the confection of sieved fruit and cream that we call a fool.

Salt

Spilt salt brings ill luck. Salt has always been an emblem of incorruptibility and was sprinkled in coffins because Satan hated it. Our word *salary* comes from the part of a Roman soldier's pay that was actually given in salt, demonstrating its importance to life. Leonardo portrayed Judas in *The Last Supper* as having knocked over the salt cellar, a significantly careless action. Three pinches of spilt salt should be thrown over the left shoulder into the face of the evil spirit that waits there for just such a careless act to give him an entrée.

Salt must never be passed from hand to hand at table, but must be put down before being taken. We say 'help to salt, help to sorrow'. The word is never uttered at sea, but some fishermen sprinkle their nets with it. It is used as a safeguard against spells by putting a few grains into the milking pail and in cradles.

Strangers

Set an extra place at table for a stranger. It is felt that this will appease the Devil in his intentions towards the household where even one of his messengers could be made welcome.

PLANTS

PLANTS

Yet again, it is helpful to think about our far off ancestor and his surroundings. From these surroundings he had to take all he could for survival purposes. Plant life provided materials like twigs for fires, wood for building, large leaves and fibres for coverings. All this in addition to the food provided by plants.

In time it will have been noticed how different plants had different properties, like comfrey that could provide leaves for infusions and balms, and seemed to have a vigorous effect on the growth of nearby vegetation. Its roots could be shredded and mixed to a paste that hardened into a cast to hold broken bones. *Such* a useful plant. What other one could be used to assist human life?

Valuable plants and crops needed safeguarding, and powers that could work beyond the limits of human powers were enlisted. Corn goddesses and tree nymphs began to be worshipped, and certain blood-thirsty and some rather jolly fertility rites were performed.

Mythology is much concerned with plant life. The Greeks were always changing their fleeing maidens into shrubs that thenceforth bore their names, and

Thor who was in charge of thunder was known to be fond of oak trees, which made it prudent to shelter under one when caught in a storm. Many plants were observed to work with the elements: tender petals shutting at sundown or under threatening skies, seeds sown when the moon was waxing germinating faster, and flowers turning their faces to the sun. Some plants inflicted stings, had nasty smells, harboured certain insects, choked their neighbours. It became easy to divide them into those possessing good and bad qualities.

Many people consider it unlucky to bring white lilac into the house, as well as the white may or blackthorn blossom. The last two are credited with having provided the Crown of Thorns, though it is unlikely that they grew in Palestine. The simple explanation is quite likely the fact that these flowers have a scent that becomes overpowering in close quarters, and may have reminded people of the scent of the lily, which is the acknowledged funeral flower. There are few trees that are not burdened with the legend of having given wood for the Cross, and Judas is said to have hanged himself from an elder. But a glance at an elder will show that it seldom has branches stout enough to support a body.

Knock on wood is one of our present-day superstitions that is most readily accepted. No one will laugh at a person who has just made a proud boast and then looks around for some wood to touch that is not teak-type plastic, even going so far as to touch his own head in mockery. This supports the idea that it is only polite to knock on the door of a wood sprite in acknowledgment of favours received.

One has only to meet an enthusiastic gardener to find a sympathetic human being. The affinity between humans and plants has come from an appreciation of both their beauty and their usefulness. We now freely talk to our plants, even shouting at them if they fail to give us good blooms or fruit. We even have electronic instruments that claim to record their sounds as they react to the way they are treated. Clearly we have to be careful how we deal with them, and much old lore exists to help us here.

Aspen

The aspen still trembles with shame as it remembers how it provided wood for the Cross. Many other trees are credited with having given wood for this purpose – cedar, cypress, elder, and olive. Considering the location of the Mount of Olives, the olive tree really is the likeliest.

Lightning

One is safe from lightning while sheltering under oak
or holly trees. The oak is Thor's favourite tree, so that
makes sense; but the holly protects by virtue of the
leaf spikes that scientifically disperse the electricity.

Touch wood

The pagan habit of thanking tree-dwelling spirits for
favours received is carried on by Christians who think
of the various sacred trees that provided wood for the
Cross.

We generally believe that pride comes before a fall,
and that to boast about something pleasant that we
expect to happen is to court disaster. So we knock on
wood to say 'thank you' in advance – just to be sure.

Mourning plants

Indoor plants will wilt if not informed of a death in
the family. A cure is to tie a strip of black cloth round
their pots so they may decently join in the mourning.
The close harmony between man and the plant world
that lies behind this practice also has the effect of
providing the bereaved with a small task that can
momentarily distract them from their introspective
sorrow.

White flowers

White may and blackthorn blossom must never be brought indoors. Children are told that their mothers will die if this is done.

Mixed red and white flowers mean death in a hospital ward. The red flowers show up starkly against the white, giving an effect of blood, and hospital workers do not wish to be reminded of blood and death any more than necessary.

Poppy

Poppies were the original cornflowers because when Ceres the Corn Goddess became so exhausted in searching for her lost daughter and neglected her duties, Somnus the God of Sleep administered poppy seed to make her sleep. Thus restored, she got on with the job of making the corn flourish. Poppies have another connection with fertility on account of the huge number of seeds they carry.

Staring into the centre of a poppy will cause temporary blindness. This is a children's belief, and has come about because the intensity of red can easily cause dazzle or blurring, particularly on a hot day.

Clover

A four-leaved clover brings exceptional luck. Eve took one with her when she was expelled from the Garden of Eden. Clover has always carried magical properties for keeping humans and animals safe from the influence of witches and fairies. It was hung by the door of the dairy to protect cows and all dairy products.

Onion

A cut onion is an unlucky thing to have in the house. This advice comes from the knowledge that onion flesh attracts and holds bacteria.

Parsley

Parsley grows best when the woman of the house wears the trousers. This statement probably comes from the belief that a parsley bed was where babies could be found, and also that unmarried pregnant girls could solve their problem by chewing the herb three times a day for three weeks.

It should only be sown on Good Friday when the soil is redeemed from the powers of Satan. Being a slow germinator it can do with such an aid to growth. It is considered to be unlucky to give parsley away direct, particularly with its root. Is this because we hesitate to part with such a valuable source of Vitamin C? An exception may be made by indicating the place where it is growing and letting the recipient help himself.

Parsley has some gloomy associations with death because the Greeks said it sprang from the blood of the hero Archemorus. They strewed it on graves and formed it into wreaths for victors in funeral games. The Romans accepted these uses and later brought the plant to Britain where it was used to cure baldness and rheumatism, and to make a strengthening eye lotion. It often happens that plants with dark qualities attributed to them become beneficial in healing.

Blackberry

Blackberries must not be gathered after 11 October. This was the old Michaelmas Day, the day on which Satan was thrown out of Heaven. He had the added misfortune of falling into a bramble bush, so took his revenge by spitting and piddling on the fruit on each anniversary of his disgrace. By this time of the year the fruit is decidedly past its best, shrivelled and spoilt by insects, so this amusing story is not essential to prevent us picking the late fruit.

Rickets, whooping-cough, and boils can be cured by making the sufferer pass through an arch of bramble that has rooted at both ends. Such arches formed by easy rooting habits, are an invitation to walk under them, and if a good reason can be found for so doing, so much the better. Jesus may have used bramble branches to sweep out the moneylenders from the Temple, if we believe one such story. Plants associated with holy stories have always been used in cures.

Marigold

Do not pick marigolds if you have not planted them yourself. Not to heed this will lead to drunkenness. Marigolds have a quality of keeping certain pests at bay, and for this reason are planted in the vegetable garden. Their power has been misinterpreted by some people who regard it as evil. I have actually met a countrywoman who adamantly refused to enter a garden where they are growing.

Mistletoe

Do not refuse a kiss under the mistletoe, and do not use it for church decoration. It was originally banned from churches because of its sacredness to Druids.

Mandrake

When a mandrake root is pulled out of the ground it gives a terrible shriek that brings immediate death to anyone hearing it. The root resembles the human form, and it would not have been difficult for this story to be believed and the plants left for the use of healers and charmers. The roots were used in the concoction of healing spells and love potions. It was possible to get round the superstition by training dogs to dig up the roots and for everyone to remain out of earshot.

Oak

A nail will cure a headache if it is first touched to the head and then hammered into the trunk of an oak tree. One particular tree was sometimes used communally by certain villages, and it was carefully protected from being cut down, for fear of all the ills being returned to their original hosts.

FURNITURE AND TOOLS

FURNITURE
AND
TOOLS

When I have made something with my hands – a patchwork quilt or an iced cake – I want people to admire it, to praise me for the workmanship and the sheer perseverance. We now have every possible aid in our handiwork, and even if we choose to use simple traditional methods and to ignore the short cuts of technology, the simplest tools will be much finer than those of the earliest generations. If I feel a need for reassurance and praise, imagine the need of the first person ever to make a spoon or a covering for the foot that might possibly resemble a shoe. The very materials and instruments used would have been of the greatest importance.

Suppose a primitive man has painstakingly managed to sharpen a flint into a cutting edge and then wedged it into a length of wood. And suppose, before he can get ready to set out on a hunt, a child gets hold of the axe and cuts himself deeply. Someone has to be blamed. And there is no doubt this early chap will, like his brothers today, be unwilling to accept responsibility. It must be the fault of evil ones. A superstition is born. Sharp edges are suspect. Now, if we receive gifts of scissors or penknives, we like to 'pay' for them to cancel out the symbolism of a wish for the friendship between giver and receiver to be cut. Even our Queen is known to hand over a token coin when given ceremonial scissors for the cutting of a tape.

Pins have a useful part to play in magic when inserted into doll images to bring about fatal effects on the human object of hate. I like the old Midlands idea that a woman can 'torment a husband or lover by wearing nine pins concealed in her dress' but omits to mention whether the gentleman in question has to be kept at arm's length!

I once broke a mirror on my birthday. It was only a small mirror, but I was secretly very upset at the prospect of seven years' bad luck. I did not then know I could have warded off the ill fortune by washing the broken pieces in a running stream, or burying them. The seven-year period is a reference to the time it takes for the cells of the body to regenerate themselves. A reflection in a mirror is thought by many Eastern races to be the face of the soul, likewise a portrait or a snapshot. A Muslim will generally hide his face if you point a camera at him.

Beds play an important part in our lives since we spends so much time in them – we are born in them, die in them, and have our wedding nights in them.

Their positioning has therefore assumed importance. The foot of a bed should never point to the door, because we only go out foot first after death. The bed of a dying person should lie parallel with the floor-boards, as if these were tracks for an easy ride to the next world. The head must, according to some, point to the magnetic North for good sleep. Bailiffs when distraining on goods will always leave the cradle alone, and many mothers know that it is a sure way to bring on another pregnancy if they give away outgrown baby furniture or prams.

The danger of walking under ladders is probably the most closely observed superstition of our present day. This may be explained away by the chance of having a pot of paint fall on one's head, or the story of the man who stepped round a ladder and into the path of a bus. A fundamental idea is that a ladder propped against a wall forms a triangle, which is a cabbalistic sign. More practically, when gibbets were in common use, ladders would be left propped against them until the body was taken down. The body was left for quite a time to act as a horrible warning, and if one passed under a ladder in the dark there might be an encounter with the dangling feet.

Chair

An overturned chair in a hospital ward heralds the arrival of a new patient.

Cradle

To rock an empty cradle portends another birth, and if a cradle is given away after a baby has outgrown it, there will soon be another arrival. It is unlucky to bring one into the house in advance of a birth.

Beds

One should not enter a bed from one side and leave it from the other. If three people help to make a bed one of them will become sick within the year. A bed turned on Sunday will cause bad dreams for the rest of the week, and in Lancashire it is considered dangerous to turn a mother's mattress until her new baby is a month old.

Airmen

Airmen in the last war never made their beds before going on a raid, because this showed they expected to return to sleep there again.

Blinds

Acorns hung at the window will keep the house safe from lightning. The Scandinavians thought that lightning could only enter through a window, and used acorns as a sop to the God Thor because he was known to have a liking for oak trees. The acorn ornament still used as a pull on window blinds is a relic of this custom.

Mirrors

Seven years' bad luck will follow the breaking of a mirror. Mirrors must be covered when there is a death in the house. Something bad will happen to you if someone looks over your shoulder into a mirror. Witches have no reflections. All these warnings are given because it is believed that a reflection is the soul.

Ladders

It is most unwise to walk under a ladder. If this cannot be avoided, the danger may be cancelled out by crossing the fingers and keeping them that way until a four-legged animal has been seen. Or one may spit on one's shoe and not look back until the spittle has dried.

Pins

See a pin, pick it up
All the day you'll have good luck.
See a pin, let it lie
All the day you'll have to cry.

Pins driven into doorposts keep witches away. A witch can be made to remove her spell by putting pins into a bottle near the fire. When they are red hot her heart will be pierced and she will be ready to do as asked. Black pins should not be used in fitting a dress, and pins that have been used to fasten a dead person's clothes must go into the coffin and never be used by the living.

Candles

An accumulation of wax dripping to one side of a candle forecasts death because it looks like a shroud. There was a 10th century Welsh law that stated a Mass could only be said when bees were present i.e. as beeswax candles. Bees are holy because they swarmed out of Paradise in disgust at the Fall of Man.

Scissors

It is unlucky to drop a pair of scissors. If they fall point down a death will soon follow, but in a dressmaker's workroom it means that business will soon increase – in the way of orders for mourning clothes.

Like gloves, dropped scissors should be picked up by someone else, and when this is done the danger is cancelled.

Opened out to form a cross they should be placed under door mats as an inhospitable gesture towards witches.

Spoon

Two spoons in a saucer indicate a wedding, and a dropped spoon a visit from a child. If it falls with the bowl uppermost it will bring a surprise, and with the bowl downward a disappointment. The first time a baby picks up a spoon it is very promising if the right hand is used. These are examples of ideas that grow up about implements in constant daily use.

Knives

Crossed knives mean a quarrel. Crossed blades are the starting position for a duel, so there is no need to look for further explanation. Knife falls, gentleman calls, is another reference to the routine of challenging.

Iron is a sure protection against bad magic as well as being the metal from which a major means of protection, a knife, is made. So we still 'pay' for gifts that have cutting edges.

Table

Do not sit on a table while talking to your lover or you will never marry each other. A warning to prevent an inelegant and unhygienic habit.

Fork

When a fork is dropped on the floor it foretells the visit of a man. If food is on the fork, the visitor will arrive with an appetite.

Kettle

A girl must never turn the spout of a steaming kettle towards the wall – not if she hopes to marry. This advice is yet another of the hundreds of precautions that girls are advised to take. Presumably, saying the wall would be damaged would not carry so much weight.

Pencils

Never use a brand new pencil when sitting an exam. This will cause failure – a nice excuse. But a pencil that is used throughout the period of preparation will remember all the answers for the examinee – a calming and confidence-producing thought.

Typewriter

If the right hand margin of typing naturally works out as evenly as the left, it means that a masterpiece has been written. I have never found this to happen for more than four lines, so obviously I have far to go!

Broom

Sweeping should be done from the sides of the room to the middle. The collected dust must be carried out of the house and not swept straight out of the door. The first warning is a question of housewifery, but the second takes note of the fact that spirits lurk outside the door and would take very strong exception to having dust thrown in their faces.

VENTURING OUT

VENTURING OUT

It is natural to feel apprehensive on the eve of a journey. Is our passport still valid? Should we have had the typhoid booster? Will the plane manage to stay in the air? We need reassurance, and we turn to superstitions that will advise on the best day of the week to travel, the right colour to wear. It is simplicity itself getting to the head of a queue for tickets at an Indian airport: one has only to bring along a fortune-teller to warn those in front that it is an inauspicious day for flying. They will vanish without question, leaving one with a certain booking and an uneasy conscience.

The way we walk, the steps we climb, the turn to the left or the right, the penalty for walking on cracks in the pavement, the consequences of going back into the house after having just left it, or of crossing some-one on the stairs – these are governed by rules that a great many people think fit to follow. My Grand-mother, for one, would always turn left out of the house, even when she wanted to go to the right. A few steps to the left would fool the evil ones, whose area this traditionally is, into believing she was going along with them. It seems a terrible waste of time, but it demonstrates the power that superstitions can have. It also shows that we actually decide which ones we want to observe and which to reject, for Grandmother had no qualms at all about walking under ladders.

We keep certain rules concerning visiting, the best known being those about first footing, when a dark-haired man has to be the first to cross the threshold of the house after midnight on New Year's Eve. In some regions the man has to have red hair, in others fair, but whichever way it is, a ceremony has to take place to ensure good fortune for the rest of the year. After all, a year is a long time in which to endure bad luck.

The ill that can result from crossing someone on the stairs must surely come from a consideration of good manners and safety. The one going up is under more stress, so the one descending *should* be the one to stand aside. But to be quite safe, one may cross fingers when such a passing is unavoidable. Some say it is unlucky to pass in silence. Unlucky or surly?

First visit

When visiting a new home it is important to take some salt, coal, and bread. These are tokens of friendship, warmth, and a full larder.

Journey

Turning back after starting out of the house is not a wise thing to do, even to fetch something that has been forgotten. It is possible to extinguish the effect by sitting down in the house, counting up to three, and then leaving a second time as if making an entirely new trip. It's those evil ones on the left who have to be fooled.

Hay cart

It augurs good luck to meet a loaded hay cart, and a wish may be made. It will be granted if silence is observed until a four-legged animal is seen – after the horse that drew the cart. The loaded cart is a sign of plenty for the coming winter, and the proviso about silence is just a test of sincerity.

Cracks

It is essential to avoid stepping on cracks between paving stones. Children believe that a bear will jump out and devour them if this rule is not meticulously kept. Contrarily, some children expect to have a bad day at school if they do *not* step on the very last crack before entering the building. Cracks between slabs were regarded as openings to graves, and to step on a grave was to call death to your family.

Children, who are so close to their feet anyway, take note of where they step and every detail of the ground around them. The game of hopscotch must surely originate from this habit.

Cushions

If a visitor plumps up the sofa cushions before leaving, it is a sign that he or she will not come again. It could possibly be taken as a criticism of one's housekeeping, but I would prefer to regard it as a nice helpful gesture in these days of rare domestic assistance, professional or otherwise.

Chair

If a visitor returns the chair he has been sitting on to its original place against the wall it means that he will not visit again. It could be argued that this is a helpful act, or that it should be left to the host.

Life-index

As long as the blade of a knife belonging to a far distant member of the family remains bright it can be assumed that all is well with him. When transportation to the Antipodes for even small crimes was common, families had little chance of receiving any communication from a member thus convicted. They resorted to keeping some of his urine tightly corked in a bottle and storing this in a safe place. As long as the liquid remained clear they felt reassured, but when it turned cloudy they put on their mourning clothes.

Snow

Walking directly in foot tracks left in the snow will bring on headaches or blindness. This sounds like advice handed out before the days when we took to wearing sun glasses for skiing.

Moon

If there is a line across the moon (i.e. a cloud streak) it will be dangerous to travel on the morrow.

SOUND

SOUND

Ancient people noting the whistling of the wind in trees took the sound to be that of the gods. Later, when they themselves learned to whistle, they felt this was a means of communication with those beings. It became a power to call up the wind. Sailors are therefore wary of whistling, and a fen dweller will not whistle for his dog at night for fear of calling up the Lantern Man – a kind of Will o' the Wisp. If he has carelessly let out a whistle, the thing to do is to lie flat on his face in the mud and allow the sprite to pass over unnoticing.

Sailors and actors are terribly worried about whistling, because their professions are precarious ones and they hate to take risks that tradition warns about. Whistling may only take place in the theatre if it forms part of the plot on stage, and an actor so far forgetting himself in the dressing room will be made to leave and turn round three times to undo the ill luck before being let in again. Actually, the sensible reasoning behind this lies in the fact that such whistling could be heard on stage and put the performers off.

The rhyme about 'a whistling woman and a

crowing hen are fit for neither God nor men', may come from the story of the woman who stood watching and whistling while the nails for the Crucifixion were being fashioned. Women in olden times were regarded as guardians of secret knowledge and therefore feared by some. Sailors usually banned them from their ships, and would have been doubly scared of one that whistled.

There are many rules of silence connected with wishing, and one will see children clapping their hands over their mouths in an effort to prevent words escaping after they have made a ritual wish. The silence is most likely to be necessary so the invoked powers can more easily hear the wish, and do something about it.

In the casting of spells the words are chanted, and this is carried forward in religious services and also in the classrooms of old-fashioned schools, where the kings of England, the rivers of France, or the verbs that take the ablative can be made to stick in the mind by chanting.

Sudden unexplained sounds call for reasons – a drinking glass that rings like a bell, the hooting of owls in daytime, furniture that creaks. We want to know why. We fear the unknown.

Words

A play will not have a long run if an usher fails to hear the opening words on a first night, neither will it succeed if the last words are spoken at the dress rehearsal. The first instance is difficult to understand, for an idle usher with few customers must be one with time to hear the opening words. The second instance is fear of the consequences of presuming that all work on the play is complete.

Wishing

A word spoken simultaneously and by accident by two people provides them with a chance to wish. They must link little fingers while wishing and not utter a word before they are unlinked.

Songs

To sing 'I dreamt I dwelt in marble halls' may bring disaster to a concert. There is a rude parody of the song which could be the result of the fear associated with it. Or perhaps singers are scared of using the wrong version in a moment of aberration. Tosti's 'Goodbye' is another ill-omened song.

Superstitions often start from hindsight, as in the

case of my Father who once had something disastrous happen to him immediately after hearing one of the 'Indian Love Lyrics'. From then on nothing would keep him from making a hasty exit if a singer started on one of these lyrics.

Glass

When a drinking glass is knocked and sets up a ringing sound, this should be blotted out as quickly as possible or a sailor will die at sea. In Norfolk it is thought that drowned people can be heard wailing their names in the wind, and the eerie ringing of the glass will call this to mind.

Death

An owl hooting in daylight portends death, and there will be death before dawn when a dog howls in the night. In Ireland and the Western Highlands of Scotland a banshee, which is a fairy-elf, announces the approach of death by a loud and terrible wailing that can only be heard by a member of the family concerned.

Rough music

Rough music, not often heard in this century, was a
form of punishment for sexual crimes in particular.
Such crimes were held to have a bad effect on a whole
tribe, or their crops, and a procession of villagers
beating on pots and pans and blowing horns would
halt from time to time to proclaim the name of the
culprit. This wretched man or woman would effec-
tively be made to pack up and leave the district.

Drake's drum

This drum that hangs in Buckland Abbey is believed
to roll of its own accord before a war. It has been
heard in 1914 and in 1918. It is very touching that a
nation should feel certain that one of its old heroes is
still on guard.

Shoes

When an actor's shoes squeak as he goes on stage he
can be sure of a good reception. For other people it
signifies that the shoes have not been paid for.

TIME

We have only to consider Stonehenge to be reminded that time, the seasons, days and hours, have pretty well always been the subject of study. The horizon on such a plain as Salisbury would have been a focal line indicating eternity beyond, and in the beyond was where men's spirits went after death to mingle with the various spirits already there. The job of the priests was to maintain good diplomatic relations with these. The sun that rose and sank over the horizon, and the stars that appeared over it at different times and places came to be seen as a pattern. The solar year was mapped out. From this came advice concerning crop cultivation, the mainstay of life.

All over the world there have been fertility rites enacted at Springtime, and numerous rules observed at other seasons. At Easter it is widely proved that eggs and bread put aside on Good Friday will remain fresh for a year. St John's Day at Midsummer is celebrated by the lighting of bonfires, with lads of the villages showing off how high and wide they can jump over the flames. Harvest time is not far away, and it will have been noted by farmers that smoke from these fires drifting over the cornfields helped to destroy harvest mites, so it is possible that farmers have been instrumental in maintaining this custom. I remember being in Italy in June and watching the St John's bonfire lit before the festivities. My Italian hostess gave me pencil and paper and told me to write down any evil thoughts I may have had about someone and then to throw the paper into the flames. A kind of shriving, a clearing out of harmful rubbish in the mind.

The month of May comes in for a great deal of superstitious thoughts, mostly with practical reasoning behind them. The best known is the one about not casting a clout 'til May be out, but there has never been agreement as to whether it is the month or the flower that is meant. However, before the calendar change of 1752, May Day was eleven days later than now, and the hawthorn would then have been in bloom. For the pragmatic, it makes sense not to throw off warm clothing at the first sign of warm sunshine and risk catching a chill if a cold spell follows. Cold *spell*? No, there is no connection, though both meanings come from Old English words.

Weather in Britain is generally changeable during May and thunderstorms are quite frequent. Thunder still strikes fear into people, whatever the scientific reasons. Primitive people must have been scared stiff and sought every possible protection. As usual, they will have turned to the gods. The very word superstition comes from the Latin *superstitio* – excessive fear of the gods – quite understandable if thunder is taken as the voice of an angry god. Do not many of us put our heads under the bedclothes and hope the storm will pass quickly?

Christmastide, which coincides with the Winter Solstice, brings with it many traditions; and throughout the countryside one will come across strange customs connected with every month of the year.

Clocks, that so obviously mark the passing of our time on earth, have been associated with superstitious ideas. My Grandfather's staff all ran screaming out of the rectory when the great clock in the hall suddenly chimed thirteen times. They took it as a certain death omen. We think of Father Time ready with his scythe at any moment, but the reign of the baby New Year lasts only a day. We are gloomy about time, getting old, dying.

Clocks

Clocks stop when their owners die. It does often occur that the watch belonging to a person who has died in the night has stopped. One may argue that the owner, so near to death, hadn't the strength to wind it properly. In other circumstances, the clocks in the deceased's house are artificially stopped, since he has no further use for finite time.

When a church clock chimes during a wedding or funeral service it is not a happy signal. In Wales it is an omen of fire if the town clock strikes during the pealing of church bells, and if the church clock strikes during a sermon this predicts a death in the parish within the week.

Sunrise

Death occurs most often just before or at sunrise. In sun-worshipping eras sacrifices to it were naturally made at sunrise, and it is held that most charms will not work unless performed at this time. It is noticeable in hospitals that births happen at inconveniently early hours, and deaths at the low hour of 3 a.m.

Moon phases

Never look at the new moon through glass. Money in the pocket should be turned. It was considered highly disrespectful to look at the Moon Goddess through the branches of trees (now translated to mean window panes), and it is salutary to be reminded how few coins one possesses.

The phases of the moon that influence tides and growth make it important to plant when it is waxing.

Moles are found to throw up more hills during this period. A waning moon gives the best time to carry out blood letting, cutting of nails, hair, and lambtails.

A new moon at the weekend will bring bad weather, and two new moons in May will bring rain for a year and a day. Sleeping with the moon shining on the face will cause lunacy, and those already mad become more violent at the time of a full moon. Children certainly suffer nightmares then, and my son could be relied upon to come running from his bed and the dragons that were chasing him.

First of the month

For good luck during the coming month say 'White Rabbits' on the first day, before uttering any other word. In some districts it is also essential to say 'Black Rabbits' the night before. Rabbits are born with open eyes and so are considered to have power over the Evil Eye. This would make them good creatures to communicate with to insure for thirty or so happy days.

Month of May

It is unlucky to marry in May. This is a leftover from the Roman festivals of the Goddess of Chastity that took place during this month. No lusty Roman would have wanted a frigid bride scared of offending this goddess. In addition, the Lemuralia were also celebrated during May. These were feasts of the dead, and likely to cast gloom around.

Wash a blanket in May
Wash a dear one away.

This warning is common in south-west England, and is similar to the famous one warning us not to throw out our warm clothes. Over zealous housewives who whip blankets off the beds too early in the year so they can be washed and stored away could cause the occupants to succumb to chills, and worse. This is a handy rhyme to prevent us from taking hasty action.

Midsummer

Bonfires lit at Midsummer will ward off spells that can ruin crops, and both the ash and the smoke will protect them until harvest time.

A rose picked on Midsummer Day and put away will still be fresh on Christmas Day. In fact, a rose kept in a dry atmosphere will retain its colour, and although it will look fresh will be dried and preserved.

Tides

Birth occurs most often with the flow of the tide and death with the ebb. This belief held mostly by shore dwellers indicates a logical train of thought.

Following on from the rhythm of tides come the statements that water boils more quickly when the tide flows, human hair must not be cut then, nor wounds dressed, and feathers of sea birds in pillows will fluff up of their own accord. The last statement could save us energy when bed-making.

Weather

To make sure of good weather for an important occasion it is important to eat up every scrap of food on the table the night before. Bits of food left lying about could attract birds, and some of those birds might be those known to bring bad weather with them.

BIRTH
AND
DEATH

BIRTH
AND
DEATH

Undoubtedly, birth and death are the two most awesome and mysterious events. Mystery makes us wonder, makes us try to find explanations and then build up sets of laws upon which we may lean in the absence of certainty. Outside forces are at work at these times, so we need the support of benign spirits. But it is all too easy when calling for such help to let in the wrong ones, because they are constantly on the lookout for souls they can snatch away from the angels. It is for this reason that we wear black at funerals, to make ourselves invisible and to cover up the fact that a death has occurred. The tolling of bells is a deterrent to bad forces, and also the lighting of candles by deathbeds and cradles. The newly-born and the newly-dead should not be left alone in a room.

After a death, perishable goods are often thrown out in case the sickness has passed into them. In Brittany, butter is placed by the body in cases where cancer is the cause of death. This is so the disease can slip into it and then be thrown out. This custom must come from the fact that cancer emits a characteristic smell and butter is all too apt to absorb smells, as anyone will know who has left some uncovered in the fridge. As a guard against witchcraft, salt is strewn in coffins because of its quality of incorruptibility and because it is hated by Satan.

To ease the pangs of birth and death, old midwives would undo all knots in clothing throughout the house and unlock all doors. Open windows would also assist the flight of the soul immediately after death.

Since we never know just when we shall die, only that death will come, we look for premonitions. Scaring things that go bump in the night seem to carry warnings. Creaking furniture, pictures crashing to the floor, birds falling down chimneys – especially black ones – are all death omens. Any bird that falls down a chimney will certainly appear black to a frightened person! I knew an Irishman who went to his landlord in a panic because a pigeon had come down the chimney in his flat. He demanded to be moved, and in those far off days it was possible to offer him another flat almost at once. He moved in great relief – but was dead within the year.

Birds

A bird flying into the house or falling down a chimney is a sign of death.

Bells

The tolling of bells will keep away bad spirits until the soul of a dead person has had time to reach the angels. After the tolling, nine strokes should follow for a man, six for a woman, and three for a child. After that should come a stroke for every year of the deceased's life.

Picture

A picture falling from its nail during the night is a sure sign of death. If it is a portrait, the omen refers to the subject.

Mistaken identity

Catching sight of a person you think you recognise and then finding you are mistaken, means death for them. This experience always brings a sense of shock.

Candles

Candles are lit by the beds of the dead and the cradles of the newborn in order to keep unwanted powers at bay.

Scapular

Small booklets containing religious writings are sometimes made from the woollen vestment of a priest to act as amulets. They are usually blessed by a priest, preferably at a shrine.

When I was six I got diphtheria and was given up by the doctor. I recall hearing voices in argument outside my room and Grandmother rushing in and pinning something woolly to my pillow. I wondered what she was doing – and suddenly felt quite bright.

Pennies

Old pennies placed on dead eyelids keep them shut until *rigor mortis* has set in. If a body is buried with open eyes it is feared that it is looking for a companion to take along. Using coins for this purpose harks back to the Greek habit of thoughtfully providing the fare to pay Charon for ferrying across the Styx.

Murder

The image of a murderer can be seen in the eyes of the victim, and that is where one should look before starting up other avenues of investigation. It has long been believed that the last thing any dead person sees is permanently imprinted on the eyeballs.

Peace

To mention a dead person's name out loud in conversation can be an unfortunate thing to do, because this can so disturb the departed spirit that it will in its turn come to cause some trouble for the living. To prevent this happening it is prudent quickly to add a phrase such as 'May she rest in peace'.

Conception

A child conceived in fine weather will be a boy, and if it is raining it will be a girl. This is perhaps because rain is like the tears that come more readily to a feminine nature.

Knife

A knife or an axe placed under the bed will cut the pain of childbirth.

Midnight

Someone born at midnight will have the power to see ghosts.

Spit

In Ireland it is customary to spit on a newborn baby to bring it luck. Saliva is universally regarded as a most precious fluid that has the power of magic and healing. Jesus cured a man of blindness by taking dust, spitting on it to form a clay which he placed on the eyelids of the sufferer.

Naming

A baby christened with the same name as that of an already dead child in the family will itself soon die. The first one will call it away.

Rainwater

If a baby's first bath is in rainwater it will start to talk early, and will never stutter.

Photograph

If three people are photographed together, the one in the middle will be the first to die.

Day of birth

Monday's child is fair of face
Tuesday's child is full of grace
Wednesday's child is full of woe
Thursday's child has far to go
Friday's child is loving and giving
Saturday's child works hard for its living
But the child that is born on the Sabbath day
is fair and wise, good and gay

This rhyme is quoted in full because we tend only to remember the lines that refer to ourselves. Just a reminder.

SUPERSTITION
IS
ALIVE
TODAY

Consideration of superstitions directs thought to the past, but the following newspaper report in the summer of 1979 demonstrates the power of cursing to be as strong as ever. A local Midlands council planned to build a motorway right through the middle of a farmer's land. He did not bother with official avenues of protest, he simply announced that he would put a curse on every workman who set foot on his land to carry out the project. The council's reaction was to cancel that particular part of the development, stating simply, 'We cannot expose our workers to such danger.'